DAILY FOCUSED DEVOTION
&
MINDFUL PRAYER

DAILY FOCUSED DEVOTION
&
MINDFUL PRAYER

This journal belongs to.

Year:

Matthew 6: 5-15
Ephesians 6:18
Philippians 4:6-7
1 Thessalonians 5:16

Julie Ann Dale

ELM HILL
A Division of
HarperCollins Christian Publishing
www.elmhillbooks.com

DAILY FOCUSED DEVOTION & MINDFUL PRAYER

Devotional Notes & Prayer Journal

Published in Nashville, Tennessee, by Elm Hill, an imprint of Thomas Nelson. Elm Hill and Thomas Nelson are registered trademarks of HarperCollins Christian Publishing, Inc.

Elm Hill titles may be purchased in bulk for educational, business, fund-raising, or sales promotional use. For information, please e-mail SpecialMarkets@ThomasNelson.com.

Library of Congress Cataloging-in-Publication Data

Library of Congress Control Number: 2020930075

ISBN 978-1-400330942 (Paperback)
ISBN 978-1-400330959 (eBook)

HOW TO USE THIS JOURNAL

DAILY DEVOTIONAL NOTES

- **DEVOTIONAL NOTES** - Strengthen your understanding of the intended message each day by writing down notes as you read or listen to the daily devotional of your choice.

- **BIBLE VERSES** - Write down the Bible verses referenced in each daily devotion.

- **KEY POINTS** - Identify key points and overall themes of each daily devotion.

- **BLESSINGS** - Enhance your faith by looking back on the prayers you listed on the same day from the week, month or year before and writing down the prayers that were answered.

- **PRAYERS** - Focus your prayer life by listing your specific requests and reviewing the blessings section before praying each day.

LIFE APPLICATIONS

The Life Applications section is alphabetized by topic so that you can easily find your favorite Bible verses when searching for faith-based answers to specific questions or needs.

- As you complete each daily devotional, you will identify Bible verses that are especially meaningful to you.

- Write down the daily devotional date, topic (i.e., marriage), and the Bible verse or verses that are helpful to you on the appropriate alphabetized page in the Life Applications section.

- Because each entry in the Life Applications section is dated, you can refer back to the notes and key points in the Daily Devotional section that apply to your specific question or need.

Daily Devotional Notes

January

CALENDAR:

SUNDAY	MONDAY	TUESDAY	WEDNESDAY	THURSDAY	FRIDAY	SATURDAY

NOTES:

DATE:

DEVOTIONAL NOTES:

BIBLE VERSES:

KEY POINTS:

BLESSINGS:

PRAYERS:

DATE:

DEVOTIONAL NOTES:

BIBLE VERSES:

KEY POINTS:

BLESSINGS:

PRAYERS:

DATE:

DEVOTIONAL NOTES:

BIBLE VERSES:

KEY POINTS:

BLESSINGS:

PRAYERS:

DATE:

DEVOTIONAL NOTES:

BIBLE VERSES:

KEY POINTS:

BLESSINGS:

PRAYERS:

DATE:

DEVOTIONAL NOTES:

BIBLE VERSES:

KEY POINTS:

BLESSINGS:

PRAYERS:

January

DATE:

DEVOTIONAL NOTES:

BIBLE VERSES:

KEY POINTS:

BLESSINGS:

PRAYERS:

DATE:

DEVOTIONAL NOTES:

BIBLE VERSES:

KEY POINTS:

BLESSINGS:

PRAYERS:

DATE:

DEVOTIONAL NOTES:

BIBLE VERSES:

KEY POINTS:

BLESSINGS:

PRAYERS:

DATE:

DEVOTIONAL NOTES:

BIBLE VERSES:

KEY POINTS:

BLESSINGS:

PRAYERS:

DATE:

DEVOTIONAL NOTES:

BIBLE VERSES:

KEY POINTS:

BLESSINGS:

PRAYERS:

DATE:

DEVOTIONAL NOTES:

BIBLE VERSES:

KEY POINTS:

BLESSINGS:

PRAYERS:

DATE:

DEVOTIONAL NOTES:

BIBLE VERSES:

KEY POINTS:

BLESSINGS:

PRAYERS:

DATE:

DEVOTIONAL NOTES:

BIBLE VERSES:

KEY POINTS:

BLESSINGS:

PRAYERS:

DATE:

DEVOTIONAL NOTES:

BIBLE VERSES:

KEY POINTS:

BLESSINGS:

PRAYERS:

DATE:

DEVOTIONAL NOTES:

BIBLE VERSES:

KEY POINTS:

BLESSINGS:

PRAYERS:

DATE:

DEVOTIONAL NOTES:

BIBLE VERSES:

KEY POINTS:

BLESSINGS:

PRAYERS:

DATE:

DEVOTIONAL NOTES:

BIBLE VERSES:

KEY POINTS:

BLESSINGS:

PRAYERS:

DATE:

DEVOTIONAL NOTES:

BIBLE VERSES:

KEY POINTS:

BLESSINGS:

PRAYERS:

DATE:

DEVOTIONAL NOTES:

BIBLE VERSES:

KEY POINTS:

BLESSINGS:

PRAYERS:

January

DATE:

DEVOTIONAL NOTES:

BIBLE VERSES:

KEY POINTS:

BLESSINGS:

PRAYERS:

DATE:

DEVOTIONAL NOTES:

BIBLE VERSES:

KEY POINTS:

BLESSINGS:

PRAYERS:

DATE:

DEVOTIONAL NOTES:

BIBLE VERSES:

KEY POINTS:

BLESSINGS:

PRAYERS:

DATE:

DEVOTIONAL NOTES:

BIBLE VERSES:

KEY POINTS:

BLESSINGS:

PRAYERS:

DATE:

DEVOTIONAL NOTES:

BIBLE VERSES:

KEY POINTS:

BLESSINGS:

PRAYERS:

DATE:

DEVOTIONAL NOTES:

BIBLE VERSES:

KEY POINTS:

BLESSINGS:

PRAYERS:

DATE:

DEVOTIONAL NOTES:

BIBLE VERSES:

KEY POINTS:

BLESSINGS:

PRAYERS:

DATE:

DEVOTIONAL NOTES:

BIBLE VERSES:

KEY POINTS:

BLESSINGS:

PRAYERS:

DATE:

DEVOTIONAL NOTES:

BIBLE VERSES:

KEY POINTS:

BLESSINGS:

PRAYERS:

DATE:

DEVOTIONAL NOTES:

BIBLE VERSES:

KEY POINTS:

BLESSINGS:

PRAYERS:

DATE:

DEVOTIONAL NOTES:

BIBLE VERSES:

KEY POINTS:

BLESSINGS:

PRAYERS:

DATE:

DEVOTIONAL NOTES:

BIBLE VERSES:

KEY POINTS:

BLESSINGS:

PRAYERS:

CALENDAR:

SUNDAY	MONDAY	TUESDAY	WEDNESDAY	THURSDAY	FRIDAY	SATURDAY

NOTES:

DATE:

DEVOTIONAL NOTES:

BIBLE VERSES:

KEY POINTS:

BLESSINGS:

PRAYERS:

DATE:

DEVOTIONAL NOTES:

BIBLE VERSES:

KEY POINTS:

BLESSINGS:

PRAYERS:

DATE:

DEVOTIONAL NOTES:

BIBLE VERSES:

KEY POINTS:

BLESSINGS:

PRAYERS:

DATE:

DEVOTIONAL NOTES:

BIBLE VERSES:

KEY POINTS:

BLESSINGS:

PRAYERS:

DATE:

DEVOTIONAL NOTES:

BIBLE VERSES:

KEY POINTS:

BLESSINGS:

PRAYERS:

February

DATE:

DEVOTIONAL NOTES:

BIBLE VERSES:

KEY POINTS:

BLESSINGS:

PRAYERS:

DATE:

DEVOTIONAL NOTES:

BIBLE VERSES:

KEY POINTS:

BLESSINGS:

PRAYERS:

DATE:

DEVOTIONAL NOTES:

BIBLE VERSES:

KEY POINTS:

BLESSINGS:

PRAYERS:

DATE:

DEVOTIONAL NOTES:

BIBLE VERSES:

KEY POINTS:

BLESSINGS:

PRAYERS:

DATE:

DEVOTIONAL NOTES:

BIBLE VERSES:

KEY POINTS:

BLESSINGS:

PRAYERS:

DATE:

DEVOTIONAL NOTES:

BIBLE VERSES:

KEY POINTS:

BLESSINGS:

PRAYERS:

DATE:

DEVOTIONAL NOTES:

BIBLE VERSES:

KEY POINTS:

BLESSINGS:

PRAYERS:

DATE:

DEVOTIONAL NOTES:

BIBLE VERSES:

KEY POINTS:

BLESSINGS:

PRAYERS:

DATE:

DEVOTIONAL NOTES:

BIBLE VERSES:

KEY POINTS:

BLESSINGS:

PRAYERS:

DATE:

DEVOTIONAL NOTES:

BIBLE VERSES:

KEY POINTS:

BLESSINGS:

PRAYERS:

February

DATE:

DEVOTIONAL NOTES:

BIBLE VERSES:

KEY POINTS:

BLESSINGS:

PRAYERS:

49

DATE:

DEVOTIONAL NOTES:

BIBLE VERSES:

KEY POINTS:

BLESSINGS:

PRAYERS:

February

DATE:

DEVOTIONAL NOTES:

BIBLE VERSES:

KEY POINTS:

BLESSINGS:

PRAYERS:

DATE:

DEVOTIONAL NOTES:

BIBLE VERSES:

KEY POINTS:

BLESSINGS:

PRAYERS:

DATE:

DEVOTIONAL NOTES:

BIBLE VERSES:

KEY POINTS:

BLESSINGS:

PRAYERS:

DATE:

DEVOTIONAL NOTES:

BIBLE VERSES:

KEY POINTS:

BLESSINGS:

PRAYERS:

February

DATE:

DEVOTIONAL NOTES:

BIBLE VERSES:

KEY POINTS:

BLESSINGS:

PRAYERS:

DATE:

DEVOTIONAL NOTES:

BIBLE VERSES:

KEY POINTS:

BLESSINGS:

PRAYERS:

DATE:

DEVOTIONAL NOTES:

BIBLE VERSES:

KEY POINTS:

BLESSINGS:

PRAYERS:

DATE:

DEVOTIONAL NOTES:

BIBLE VERSES:

KEY POINTS:

BLESSINGS:

PRAYERS:

February

DATE:

DEVOTIONAL NOTES:

BIBLE VERSES:

KEY POINTS:

BLESSINGS:

PRAYERS:

DATE:

DEVOTIONAL NOTES:

BIBLE VERSES:

KEY POINTS:

BLESSINGS:

PRAYERS:

February

DATE:

DEVOTIONAL NOTES:

BIBLE VERSES:

KEY POINTS:

BLESSINGS:

PRAYERS:

DATE:

DEVOTIONAL NOTES:

BIBLE VERSES:

KEY POINTS:

BLESSINGS:

PRAYERS:

CALENDAR:

SUNDAY	MONDAY	TUESDAY	WEDNESDAY	THURSDAY	FRIDAY	SATURDAY

NOTES:

DATE:

DEVOTIONAL NOTES:

BIBLE VERSES:

KEY POINTS:

BLESSINGS:

PRAYERS:

DATE:

DEVOTIONAL NOTES:

BIBLE VERSES:

KEY POINTS:

BLESSINGS:

PRAYERS:

DATE:

DEVOTIONAL NOTES:

BIBLE VERSES:

KEY POINTS:

BLESSINGS:

PRAYERS:

DATE:

DEVOTIONAL NOTES:

BIBLE VERSES:

KEY POINTS:

BLESSINGS:

PRAYERS:

DATE:

DEVOTIONAL NOTES:

BIBLE VERSES:

KEY POINTS:

BLESSINGS:

PRAYERS:

March

DATE:

DEVOTIONAL NOTES:

BIBLE VERSES:

KEY POINTS:

BLESSINGS:

PRAYERS:

DATE:

DEVOTIONAL NOTES:

BIBLE VERSES:

KEY POINTS:

BLESSINGS:

PRAYERS:

March

DATE:

DEVOTIONAL NOTES:

BIBLE VERSES:

KEY POINTS:

BLESSINGS:

PRAYERS:

DATE:

DEVOTIONAL NOTES:

BIBLE VERSES:

KEY POINTS:

BLESSINGS:

PRAYERS:

March

DATE:

DEVOTIONAL NOTES:

BIBLE VERSES:

KEY POINTS:

BLESSINGS:

PRAYERS:

DATE:

DEVOTIONAL NOTES:

BIBLE VERSES:

KEY POINTS:

BLESSINGS:

PRAYERS:

March

DATE:

DEVOTIONAL NOTES:

BIBLE VERSES:

KEY POINTS:

BLESSINGS:

PRAYERS:

DATE:

DEVOTIONAL NOTES:

BIBLE VERSES:

KEY POINTS:

BLESSINGS:

PRAYERS:

DATE:

DEVOTIONAL NOTES:

BIBLE VERSES:

KEY POINTS:

BLESSINGS:

PRAYERS:

DATE:

DEVOTIONAL NOTES:

BIBLE VERSES:

KEY POINTS:

BLESSINGS:

PRAYERS:

DATE:

DEVOTIONAL NOTES:

BIBLE VERSES:

KEY POINTS:

BLESSINGS:

PRAYERS:

DATE:

DEVOTIONAL NOTES:

BIBLE VERSES:

KEY POINTS:

BLESSINGS:

PRAYERS:

March

DATE:

DEVOTIONAL NOTES:

BIBLE VERSES:

KEY POINTS:

BLESSINGS:

PRAYERS:

DATE:

DEVOTIONAL NOTES:

BIBLE VERSES:

KEY POINTS:

BLESSINGS:

PRAYERS:

March

DATE:

DEVOTIONAL NOTES:

BIBLE VERSES:

KEY POINTS:

BLESSINGS:

PRAYERS:

DATE:

DEVOTIONAL NOTES:

BIBLE VERSES:

KEY POINTS:

BLESSINGS:

PRAYERS:

March

DATE:

DEVOTIONAL NOTES:

BIBLE VERSES:

KEY POINTS:

BLESSINGS:

PRAYERS:

DATE:

DEVOTIONAL NOTES:

BIBLE VERSES:

KEY POINTS:

BLESSINGS:

PRAYERS:

DATE:

DEVOTIONAL NOTES:

BIBLE VERSES:

KEY POINTS:

BLESSINGS:

PRAYERS:

DATE:

DEVOTIONAL NOTES:

BIBLE VERSES:

KEY POINTS:

BLESSINGS:

PRAYERS:

March

DATE:

DEVOTIONAL NOTES:

BIBLE VERSES:

KEY POINTS:

BLESSINGS:

PRAYERS:

DATE:

DEVOTIONAL NOTES:

BIBLE VERSES:

KEY POINTS:

BLESSINGS:

PRAYERS:

DATE:

DEVOTIONAL NOTES:

BIBLE VERSES:

KEY POINTS:

BLESSINGS:

PRAYERS:

DATE:

DEVOTIONAL NOTES:

BIBLE VERSES:

KEY POINTS:

BLESSINGS:

PRAYERS:

DATE:

DEVOTIONAL NOTES:

BIBLE VERSES:

KEY POINTS:

BLESSINGS:

PRAYERS:

DATE:

DEVOTIONAL NOTES:

BIBLE VERSES:

KEY POINTS:

BLESSINGS:

PRAYERS:

CALENDAR:

SUNDAY	MONDAY	TUESDAY	WEDNESDAY	THURSDAY	FRIDAY	SATURDAY

NOTES:

DATE:

DEVOTIONAL NOTES:

BIBLE VERSES:

KEY POINTS:

BLESSINGS:

PRAYERS:

DATE:

DEVOTIONAL NOTES:

BIBLE VERSES:

KEY POINTS:

BLESSINGS:

PRAYERS:

DATE:

DEVOTIONAL NOTES:

BIBLE VERSES:

KEY POINTS:

BLESSINGS:

PRAYERS:

DATE:

DEVOTIONAL NOTES:

BIBLE VERSES:

KEY POINTS:

BLESSINGS:

PRAYERS:

DATE:

DEVOTIONAL NOTES:

BIBLE VERSES:

KEY POINTS:

BLESSINGS:

PRAYERS:

DATE:

DEVOTIONAL NOTES:

BIBLE VERSES:

KEY POINTS:

BLESSINGS:

PRAYERS:

DATE:

DEVOTIONAL NOTES:

BIBLE VERSES:

KEY POINTS:

BLESSINGS:

PRAYERS:

DATE:

DEVOTIONAL NOTES:

BIBLE VERSES:

KEY POINTS:

BLESSINGS:

PRAYERS:

DATE:

DEVOTIONAL NOTES:

BIBLE VERSES:

KEY POINTS:

BLESSINGS:

PRAYERS:

DATE:

DEVOTIONAL NOTES:

BIBLE VERSES:

KEY POINTS:

BLESSINGS:

PRAYERS:

DATE:

DEVOTIONAL NOTES:

BIBLE VERSES:

KEY POINTS:

BLESSINGS:

PRAYERS:

DATE:

DEVOTIONAL NOTES:

BIBLE VERSES:

KEY POINTS:

BLESSINGS:

PRAYERS:

DATE:

DEVOTIONAL NOTES:

BIBLE VERSES:

KEY POINTS:

BLESSINGS:

PRAYERS:

DATE:

DEVOTIONAL NOTES:

BIBLE VERSES:

KEY POINTS:

BLESSINGS:

PRAYERS:

DATE:

DEVOTIONAL NOTES:

BIBLE VERSES:

KEY POINTS:

BLESSINGS:

PRAYERS:

DATE:

DEVOTIONAL NOTES:

BIBLE VERSES:

KEY POINTS:

BLESSINGS:

PRAYERS:

DATE:

DEVOTIONAL NOTES:

BIBLE VERSES:

KEY POINTS:

BLESSINGS:

PRAYERS:

DATE:

DEVOTIONAL NOTES:

BIBLE VERSES:

KEY POINTS:

BLESSINGS:

PRAYERS:

DATE:

DEVOTIONAL NOTES:

BIBLE VERSES:

KEY POINTS:

BLESSINGS:

PRAYERS:

DATE:

DEVOTIONAL NOTES:

BIBLE VERSES:

KEY POINTS:

BLESSINGS:

PRAYERS:

DATE:

DEVOTIONAL NOTES:

BIBLE VERSES:

KEY POINTS:

BLESSINGS:

PRAYERS:

April

DATE:

DEVOTIONAL NOTES:

BIBLE VERSES:

KEY POINTS:

BLESSINGS:

PRAYERS:

117

DATE:

DEVOTIONAL NOTES:

BIBLE VERSES:

KEY POINTS:

BLESSINGS:

PRAYERS:

DATE:

DEVOTIONAL NOTES:

BIBLE VERSES:

KEY POINTS:

BLESSINGS:

PRAYERS:

DATE:

DEVOTIONAL NOTES:

BIBLE VERSES:

KEY POINTS:

BLESSINGS:

PRAYERS:

DATE:

DEVOTIONAL NOTES:

BIBLE VERSES:

KEY POINTS:

BLESSINGS:

PRAYERS:

DATE:

DEVOTIONAL NOTES:

BIBLE VERSES:

KEY POINTS:

BLESSINGS:

PRAYERS:

April

DATE:

DEVOTIONAL NOTES:

BIBLE VERSES:

KEY POINTS:

BLESSINGS:

PRAYERS:

123

DATE:

DEVOTIONAL NOTES:

BIBLE VERSES:

KEY POINTS:

BLESSINGS:

PRAYERS:

DATE:

DEVOTIONAL NOTES:

BIBLE VERSES:

KEY POINTS:

BLESSINGS:

PRAYERS:

DATE:

DEVOTIONAL NOTES:

BIBLE VERSES:

KEY POINTS:

BLESSINGS:

PRAYERS:

May

CALENDAR:

SUNDAY	MONDAY	TUESDAY	WEDNESDAY	THURSDAY	FRIDAY	SATURDAY

NOTES:

DATE:

DEVOTIONAL NOTES:

BIBLE VERSES:

KEY POINTS:

BLESSINGS:

PRAYERS:

DATE:

DEVOTIONAL NOTES:

BIBLE VERSES:

KEY POINTS:

BLESSINGS:

PRAYERS:

DATE:

DEVOTIONAL NOTES:

BIBLE VERSES:

KEY POINTS:

BLESSINGS:

PRAYERS:

May

DATE:

DEVOTIONAL NOTES:

BIBLE VERSES:

KEY POINTS:

BLESSINGS:

PRAYERS:

DATE:

DEVOTIONAL NOTES:

BIBLE VERSES:

KEY POINTS:

BLESSINGS:

PRAYERS:

May

DATE:

DEVOTIONAL NOTES:

BIBLE VERSES:

KEY POINTS:

BLESSINGS:

PRAYERS:

DATE:

DEVOTIONAL NOTES:

BIBLE VERSES:

KEY POINTS:

BLESSINGS:

PRAYERS:

May

DATE:

DEVOTIONAL NOTES:

BIBLE VERSES:

KEY POINTS:

BLESSINGS:

PRAYERS:

DATE:

DEVOTIONAL NOTES:

BIBLE VERSES:

KEY POINTS:

BLESSINGS:

PRAYERS:

DATE:

DEVOTIONAL NOTES:

BIBLE VERSES:

KEY POINTS:

BLESSINGS:

PRAYERS:

DATE:

DEVOTIONAL NOTES:

BIBLE VERSES:

KEY POINTS:

BLESSINGS:

PRAYERS:

DATE:

DEVOTIONAL NOTES:

BIBLE VERSES:

KEY POINTS:

BLESSINGS:

PRAYERS:

DATE:

DEVOTIONAL NOTES:

BIBLE VERSES:

KEY POINTS:

BLESSINGS:

PRAYERS:

DATE:

DEVOTIONAL NOTES:

BIBLE VERSES:

KEY POINTS:

BLESSINGS:

PRAYERS:

DATE:

DEVOTIONAL NOTES:

BIBLE VERSES:

KEY POINTS:

BLESSINGS:

PRAYERS:

DATE:

DEVOTIONAL NOTES:

BIBLE VERSES:

KEY POINTS:

BLESSINGS:

PRAYERS:

DATE:

DEVOTIONAL NOTES:

BIBLE VERSES:

KEY POINTS:

BLESSINGS:

PRAYERS:

144

DATE:

DEVOTIONAL NOTES:

BIBLE VERSES:

KEY POINTS:

BLESSINGS:

PRAYERS:

DATE:

DEVOTIONAL NOTES:

BIBLE VERSES:

KEY POINTS:

BLESSINGS:

PRAYERS:

DATE:

DEVOTIONAL NOTES:

BIBLE VERSES:

KEY POINTS:

BLESSINGS:

PRAYERS:

DATE:

DEVOTIONAL NOTES:

BIBLE VERSES:

KEY POINTS:

BLESSINGS:

PRAYERS:

DATE:

DEVOTIONAL NOTES:

BIBLE VERSES:

KEY POINTS:

BLESSINGS:

PRAYERS:

DATE:

DEVOTIONAL NOTES:

BIBLE VERSES:

KEY POINTS:

BLESSINGS:

PRAYERS:

May

DATE:

DEVOTIONAL NOTES:

BIBLE VERSES:

KEY POINTS:

BLESSINGS:

PRAYERS:

DATE:

DEVOTIONAL NOTES:

BIBLE VERSES:

KEY POINTS:

BLESSINGS:

PRAYERS:

DATE:

DEVOTIONAL NOTES:

BIBLE VERSES:

KEY POINTS:

BLESSINGS:

PRAYERS:

DATE:

DEVOTIONAL NOTES:

BIBLE VERSES:

KEY POINTS:

BLESSINGS:

PRAYERS:

DATE:

DEVOTIONAL NOTES:

BIBLE VERSES:

KEY POINTS:

BLESSINGS:

PRAYERS:

DATE:

DEVOTIONAL NOTES:

BIBLE VERSES:

KEY POINTS:

BLESSINGS:

PRAYERS:

May

DATE:

DEVOTIONAL NOTES:

BIBLE VERSES:

KEY POINTS:

BLESSINGS:

PRAYERS:

DATE:

DEVOTIONAL NOTES:

BIBLE VERSES:

KEY POINTS:

BLESSINGS:

PRAYERS:

June

CALENDAR:

SUNDAY	MONDAY	TUESDAY	WEDNESDAY	THURSDAY	FRIDAY	SATURDAY

NOTES:

DATE:

DEVOTIONAL NOTES:

BIBLE VERSES:

KEY POINTS:

BLESSINGS:

PRAYERS:

DATE:

DEVOTIONAL NOTES:

BIBLE VERSES:

KEY POINTS:

BLESSINGS:

PRAYERS:

DATE:

DEVOTIONAL NOTES:

BIBLE VERSES:

KEY POINTS:

BLESSINGS:

PRAYERS:

DATE:

DEVOTIONAL NOTES:

BIBLE VERSES:

KEY POINTS:

BLESSINGS:

PRAYERS:

DATE:

DEVOTIONAL NOTES:

BIBLE VERSES:

KEY POINTS:

BLESSINGS:

PRAYERS:

June

DATE:

DEVOTIONAL NOTES:

BIBLE VERSES:

KEY POINTS:

BLESSINGS:

PRAYERS:

DATE:

DEVOTIONAL NOTES:

BIBLE VERSES:

KEY POINTS:

BLESSINGS:

PRAYERS:

June

DATE:

DEVOTIONAL NOTES:

BIBLE VERSES:

KEY POINTS:

BLESSINGS:

PRAYERS:

DATE:

DEVOTIONAL NOTES:

BIBLE VERSES:

KEY POINTS:

BLESSINGS:

PRAYERS:

June

DATE:

DEVOTIONAL NOTES:

BIBLE VERSES:

KEY POINTS:

BLESSINGS:

PRAYERS:

DATE:

DEVOTIONAL NOTES:

BIBLE VERSES:

KEY POINTS:

BLESSINGS:

PRAYERS:

DATE:

DEVOTIONAL NOTES:

BIBLE VERSES:

KEY POINTS:

BLESSINGS:

PRAYERS:

DATE:

DEVOTIONAL NOTES:

BIBLE VERSES:

KEY POINTS:

BLESSINGS:

PRAYERS:

June

DATE:

DEVOTIONAL NOTES:

BIBLE VERSES:

KEY POINTS:

BLESSINGS:

PRAYERS:

DATE:

DEVOTIONAL NOTES:

BIBLE VERSES:

KEY POINTS:

BLESSINGS:

PRAYERS:

DATE:

DEVOTIONAL NOTES:

BIBLE VERSES:

KEY POINTS:

BLESSINGS:

PRAYERS:

DATE:

DEVOTIONAL NOTES:

BIBLE VERSES:

KEY POINTS:

BLESSINGS:

PRAYERS:

DATE:

DEVOTIONAL NOTES:

BIBLE VERSES:

KEY POINTS:

BLESSINGS:

PRAYERS:

DATE:

DEVOTIONAL NOTES:

BIBLE VERSES:

KEY POINTS:

BLESSINGS:

PRAYERS:

DATE:

DEVOTIONAL NOTES:

BIBLE VERSES:

KEY POINTS:

BLESSINGS:

PRAYERS:

DATE:

DEVOTIONAL NOTES:

BIBLE VERSES:

KEY POINTS:

BLESSINGS:

PRAYERS:

June

DATE:

DEVOTIONAL NOTES:

BIBLE VERSES:

KEY POINTS:

BLESSINGS:

PRAYERS:

DATE:

DEVOTIONAL NOTES:

BIBLE VERSES:

KEY POINTS:

BLESSINGS:

PRAYERS:

DATE:

DEVOTIONAL NOTES:

BIBLE VERSES:

KEY POINTS:

BLESSINGS:

PRAYERS:

DATE:

DEVOTIONAL NOTES:

BIBLE VERSES:

KEY POINTS:

BLESSINGS:

PRAYERS:

DATE:

DEVOTIONAL NOTES:

BIBLE VERSES:

KEY POINTS:

BLESSINGS:

PRAYERS:

DATE:

DEVOTIONAL NOTES:

BIBLE VERSES:

KEY POINTS:

BLESSINGS:

PRAYERS:

June

DATE:

DEVOTIONAL NOTES:

BIBLE VERSES:

KEY POINTS:

BLESSINGS:

PRAYERS:

DATE:

DEVOTIONAL NOTES:

BIBLE VERSES:

KEY POINTS:

BLESSINGS:

PRAYERS:

DATE:

DEVOTIONAL NOTES:

BIBLE VERSES:

KEY POINTS:

BLESSINGS:

PRAYERS:

DATE:

DEVOTIONAL NOTES:

BIBLE VERSES:

KEY POINTS:

BLESSINGS:

PRAYERS:

CALENDAR:

SUNDAY	MONDAY	TUESDAY	WEDNESDAY	THURSDAY	FRIDAY	SATURDAY

NOTES:

DATE:

DEVOTIONAL NOTES:

BIBLE VERSES:

KEY POINTS:

BLESSINGS:

PRAYERS:

DATE:

DEVOTIONAL NOTES:

BIBLE VERSES:

KEY POINTS:

BLESSINGS:

PRAYERS:

DATE:

DEVOTIONAL NOTES:

BIBLE VERSES:

KEY POINTS:

BLESSINGS:

PRAYERS:

DATE:

DEVOTIONAL NOTES:

BIBLE VERSES:

KEY POINTS:

BLESSINGS:

PRAYERS:

DATE:

DEVOTIONAL NOTES:

BIBLE VERSES:

KEY POINTS:

BLESSINGS:

PRAYERS:

DATE:

DEVOTIONAL NOTES:

BIBLE VERSES:

KEY POINTS:

BLESSINGS:

PRAYERS:

DATE:

DEVOTIONAL NOTES:

BIBLE VERSES:

KEY POINTS:

BLESSINGS:

PRAYERS:

July

DATE:

DEVOTIONAL NOTES:

BIBLE VERSES:

KEY POINTS:

BLESSINGS:

PRAYERS:

DATE:

DEVOTIONAL NOTES:

BIBLE VERSES:

KEY POINTS:

BLESSINGS:

PRAYERS:

DATE:

DEVOTIONAL NOTES:

BIBLE VERSES:

KEY POINTS:

BLESSINGS:

PRAYERS:

DATE:

DEVOTIONAL NOTES:

BIBLE VERSES:

KEY POINTS:

BLESSINGS:

PRAYERS:

July

DATE:

DEVOTIONAL NOTES:

BIBLE VERSES:

KEY POINTS:

BLESSINGS:

PRAYERS:

DATE:

DEVOTIONAL NOTES:

BIBLE VERSES:

KEY POINTS:

BLESSINGS:

PRAYERS:

DATE:

DEVOTIONAL NOTES:

BIBLE VERSES:

KEY POINTS:

BLESSINGS:

PRAYERS:

DATE:

DEVOTIONAL NOTES:

BIBLE VERSES:

KEY POINTS:

BLESSINGS:

PRAYERS:

July

DATE:

DEVOTIONAL NOTES:

BIBLE VERSES:

KEY POINTS:

BLESSINGS:

PRAYERS:

DATE:

DEVOTIONAL NOTES:

BIBLE VERSES:

KEY POINTS:

BLESSINGS:

PRAYERS:

July

DATE:

DEVOTIONAL NOTES:

BIBLE VERSES:

KEY POINTS:

BLESSINGS:

PRAYERS:

DATE:

DEVOTIONAL NOTES:

BIBLE VERSES:

KEY POINTS:

BLESSINGS:

PRAYERS:

DATE:

DEVOTIONAL NOTES:

BIBLE VERSES:

KEY POINTS:

BLESSINGS:

PRAYERS:

DATE:

DEVOTIONAL NOTES:

BIBLE VERSES:

KEY POINTS:

BLESSINGS:

PRAYERS:

DATE:

DEVOTIONAL NOTES:

BIBLE VERSES:

KEY POINTS:

BLESSINGS:

PRAYERS:

DATE:

DEVOTIONAL NOTES:

BIBLE VERSES:

KEY POINTS:

BLESSINGS:

PRAYERS:

DATE:

DEVOTIONAL NOTES:

BIBLE VERSES:

KEY POINTS:

BLESSINGS:

PRAYERS:

DATE:

DEVOTIONAL NOTES:

BIBLE VERSES:

KEY POINTS:

BLESSINGS:

PRAYERS:

DATE:

DEVOTIONAL NOTES:

BIBLE VERSES:

KEY POINTS:

BLESSINGS:

PRAYERS:

DATE:

DEVOTIONAL NOTES:

BIBLE VERSES:

KEY POINTS:

BLESSINGS:

PRAYERS:

DATE:

DEVOTIONAL NOTES:

BIBLE VERSES:

KEY POINTS:

BLESSINGS:

PRAYERS:

DATE:

DEVOTIONAL NOTES:

BIBLE VERSES:

KEY POINTS:

BLESSINGS:

PRAYERS:

DATE:

DEVOTIONAL NOTES:

BIBLE VERSES:

KEY POINTS:

BLESSINGS:

PRAYERS:

DATE:

DEVOTIONAL NOTES:

BIBLE VERSES:

KEY POINTS:

BLESSINGS:

PRAYERS:

August

CALENDAR:

SUNDAY	MONDAY	TUESDAY	WEDNESDAY	THURSDAY	FRIDAY	SATURDAY

NOTES:

DATE:

DEVOTIONAL NOTES:

BIBLE VERSES:

KEY POINTS:

BLESSINGS:

PRAYERS:

DATE:

DEVOTIONAL NOTES:

BIBLE VERSES:

KEY POINTS:

BLESSINGS:

PRAYERS:

DATE:

DEVOTIONAL NOTES:

BIBLE VERSES:

KEY POINTS:

BLESSINGS:

PRAYERS:

August

DATE:

DEVOTIONAL NOTES:

BIBLE VERSES:

KEY POINTS:

BLESSINGS:

PRAYERS:

DATE:

DEVOTIONAL NOTES:

BIBLE VERSES:

KEY POINTS:

BLESSINGS:

PRAYERS:

DATE:

DEVOTIONAL NOTES:

BIBLE VERSES:

KEY POINTS:

BLESSINGS:

PRAYERS:

DATE:

DEVOTIONAL NOTES:

BIBLE VERSES:

KEY POINTS:

BLESSINGS:

PRAYERS:

DATE:

DEVOTIONAL NOTES:

BIBLE VERSES:

KEY POINTS:

BLESSINGS:

PRAYERS:

DATE:

DEVOTIONAL NOTES:

BIBLE VERSES:

KEY POINTS:

BLESSINGS:

PRAYERS:

DATE:

DEVOTIONAL NOTES:

BIBLE VERSES:

KEY POINTS:

BLESSINGS:

PRAYERS:

DATE:

DEVOTIONAL NOTES:

BIBLE VERSES:

KEY POINTS:

BLESSINGS:

PRAYERS:

DATE:

DEVOTIONAL NOTES:

BIBLE VERSES:

KEY POINTS:

BLESSINGS:

PRAYERS:

DATE:

DEVOTIONAL NOTES:

BIBLE VERSES:

KEY POINTS:

BLESSINGS:

PRAYERS:

DATE:

DEVOTIONAL NOTES:

BIBLE VERSES:

KEY POINTS:

BLESSINGS:

PRAYERS:

DATE:

DEVOTIONAL NOTES:

BIBLE VERSES:

KEY POINTS:

BLESSINGS:

PRAYERS:

DATE:

DEVOTIONAL NOTES:

BIBLE VERSES:

KEY POINTS:

BLESSINGS:

PRAYERS:

DATE:

DEVOTIONAL NOTES:

BIBLE VERSES:

KEY POINTS:

BLESSINGS:

PRAYERS:

DATE:

DEVOTIONAL NOTES:

BIBLE VERSES:

KEY POINTS:

BLESSINGS:

PRAYERS:

DATE:

DEVOTIONAL NOTES:

BIBLE VERSES:

KEY POINTS:

BLESSINGS:

PRAYERS:

DATE:

DEVOTIONAL NOTES:

BIBLE VERSES:

KEY POINTS:

BLESSINGS:

PRAYERS:

DATE:

DEVOTIONAL NOTES:

BIBLE VERSES:

KEY POINTS:

BLESSINGS:

PRAYERS:

August

DATE:

DEVOTIONAL NOTES:

BIBLE VERSES:

KEY POINTS:

BLESSINGS:

PRAYERS:

DATE:

DEVOTIONAL NOTES:

BIBLE VERSES:

KEY POINTS:

BLESSINGS:

PRAYERS:

DATE:

DEVOTIONAL NOTES:

BIBLE VERSES:

KEY POINTS:

BLESSINGS:

PRAYERS:

DATE:

DEVOTIONAL NOTES:

BIBLE VERSES:

KEY POINTS:

BLESSINGS:

PRAYERS:

DATE:

DEVOTIONAL NOTES:

BIBLE VERSES:

KEY POINTS:

BLESSINGS:

PRAYERS:

DATE:

DEVOTIONAL NOTES:

BIBLE VERSES:

KEY POINTS:

BLESSINGS:

PRAYERS:

DATE:

DEVOTIONAL NOTES:

BIBLE VERSES:

KEY POINTS:

BLESSINGS:

PRAYERS:

DATE:

DEVOTIONAL NOTES:

BIBLE VERSES:

KEY POINTS:

BLESSINGS:

PRAYERS:

DATE:

DEVOTIONAL NOTES:

BIBLE VERSES:

KEY POINTS:

BLESSINGS:

PRAYERS:

DATE:

DEVOTIONAL NOTES:

BIBLE VERSES:

KEY POINTS:

BLESSINGS:

PRAYERS:

September

SUNDAY	MONDAY	TUESDAY	WEDNESDAY	THURSDAY	FRIDAY	SATURDAY

NOTES:

DATE:

DEVOTIONAL NOTES:

BIBLE VERSES:

KEY POINTS:

BLESSINGS:

PRAYERS:

DATE:

DEVOTIONAL NOTES:

BIBLE VERSES:

KEY POINTS:

BLESSINGS:

PRAYERS:

DATE:

DEVOTIONAL NOTES:

BIBLE VERSES:

KEY POINTS:

BLESSINGS:

PRAYERS:

DATE:

DEVOTIONAL NOTES:

BIBLE VERSES:

KEY POINTS:

BLESSINGS:

PRAYERS:

DATE:

DEVOTIONAL NOTES:

BIBLE VERSES:

KEY POINTS:

BLESSINGS:

PRAYERS:

September

DATE:

DEVOTIONAL NOTES:

BIBLE VERSES:

KEY POINTS:

BLESSINGS:

PRAYERS:

DATE:

DEVOTIONAL NOTES:

BIBLE VERSES:

KEY POINTS:

BLESSINGS:

PRAYERS:

DATE:

DEVOTIONAL NOTES:

BIBLE VERSES:

KEY POINTS:

BLESSINGS:

PRAYERS:

DATE:

DEVOTIONAL NOTES:

BIBLE VERSES:

KEY POINTS:

BLESSINGS:

PRAYERS:

DATE:

DEVOTIONAL NOTES:

BIBLE VERSES:

KEY POINTS:

BLESSINGS:

PRAYERS:

DATE:

DEVOTIONAL NOTES:

BIBLE VERSES:

KEY POINTS:

BLESSINGS:

PRAYERS:

DATE:

DEVOTIONAL NOTES:

BIBLE VERSES:

KEY POINTS:

BLESSINGS:

PRAYERS:

DATE:

DEVOTIONAL NOTES:

BIBLE VERSES:

KEY POINTS:

BLESSINGS:

PRAYERS:

September

DATE:

DEVOTIONAL NOTES:

BIBLE VERSES:

KEY POINTS:

BLESSINGS:

PRAYERS:

DATE:

DEVOTIONAL NOTES:

BIBLE VERSES:

KEY POINTS:

BLESSINGS:

PRAYERS:

DATE:

DEVOTIONAL NOTES:

BIBLE VERSES:

KEY POINTS:

BLESSINGS:

PRAYERS:

DATE:

DEVOTIONAL NOTES:

BIBLE VERSES:

KEY POINTS:

BLESSINGS:

PRAYERS:

DATE:

DEVOTIONAL NOTES:

BIBLE VERSES:

KEY POINTS:

BLESSINGS:

PRAYERS:

DATE:

DEVOTIONAL NOTES:

BIBLE VERSES:

KEY POINTS:

BLESSINGS:

PRAYERS:

September

DATE:

DEVOTIONAL NOTES:

BIBLE VERSES:

KEY POINTS:

BLESSINGS:

PRAYERS:

DATE:

DEVOTIONAL NOTES:

BIBLE VERSES:

KEY POINTS:

BLESSINGS:

PRAYERS:

DATE:

DEVOTIONAL NOTES:

BIBLE VERSES:

KEY POINTS:

BLESSINGS:

PRAYERS:

DATE:

DEVOTIONAL NOTES:

BIBLE VERSES:

KEY POINTS:

BLESSINGS:

PRAYERS:

September

DATE:

DEVOTIONAL NOTES:

BIBLE VERSES:

KEY POINTS:

BLESSINGS:

PRAYERS:

DATE:

DEVOTIONAL NOTES:

BIBLE VERSES:

KEY POINTS:

BLESSINGS:

PRAYERS:

September

DATE:

DEVOTIONAL NOTES:

BIBLE VERSES:

KEY POINTS:

BLESSINGS:

PRAYERS:

DATE:

DEVOTIONAL NOTES:

BIBLE VERSES:

KEY POINTS:

BLESSINGS:

PRAYERS:

DATE:

DEVOTIONAL NOTES:

BIBLE VERSES:

KEY POINTS:

BLESSINGS:

PRAYERS:

DATE:

DEVOTIONAL NOTES:

BIBLE VERSES:

KEY POINTS:

BLESSINGS:

PRAYERS:

DATE:

DEVOTIONAL NOTES:

BIBLE VERSES:

KEY POINTS:

BLESSINGS:

PRAYERS:

DATE:

DEVOTIONAL NOTES:

BIBLE VERSES:

KEY POINTS:

BLESSINGS:

PRAYERS:

October

CALENDAR:

SUNDAY	MONDAY	TUESDAY	WEDNESDAY	THURSDAY	FRIDAY	SATURDAY

NOTES:

DATE:

DEVOTIONAL NOTES:

BIBLE VERSES:

KEY POINTS:

BLESSINGS:

PRAYERS:

DATE:

DEVOTIONAL NOTES:

BIBLE VERSES:

KEY POINTS:

BLESSINGS:

PRAYERS:

DATE:

DEVOTIONAL NOTES:

BIBLE VERSES:

KEY POINTS:

BLESSINGS:

PRAYERS:

DATE:

DEVOTIONAL NOTES:

BIBLE VERSES:

KEY POINTS:

BLESSINGS:

PRAYERS:

DATE:

DEVOTIONAL NOTES:

BIBLE VERSES:

KEY POINTS:

BLESSINGS:

PRAYERS:

DATE:

DEVOTIONAL NOTES:

BIBLE VERSES:

KEY POINTS:

BLESSINGS:

PRAYERS:

DATE:

DEVOTIONAL NOTES:

BIBLE VERSES:

KEY POINTS:

BLESSINGS:

PRAYERS:

DATE:

DEVOTIONAL NOTES:

BIBLE VERSES:

KEY POINTS:

BLESSINGS:

PRAYERS:

DATE:

DEVOTIONAL NOTES:

BIBLE VERSES:

KEY POINTS:

BLESSINGS:

PRAYERS:

DATE:

DEVOTIONAL NOTES:

BIBLE VERSES:

KEY POINTS:

BLESSINGS:

PRAYERS:

DATE:

DEVOTIONAL NOTES:

BIBLE VERSES:

KEY POINTS:

BLESSINGS:

PRAYERS:

October

DATE:

DEVOTIONAL NOTES:

BIBLE VERSES:

KEY POINTS:

BLESSINGS:

PRAYERS:

DATE:

DEVOTIONAL NOTES:

BIBLE VERSES:

KEY POINTS:

BLESSINGS:

PRAYERS:

October

DATE:

DEVOTIONAL NOTES:

BIBLE VERSES:

KEY POINTS:

BLESSINGS:

PRAYERS:

DATE:

DEVOTIONAL NOTES:

BIBLE VERSES:

KEY POINTS:

BLESSINGS:

PRAYERS:

DATE:

DEVOTIONAL NOTES:

BIBLE VERSES:

KEY POINTS:

BLESSINGS:

PRAYERS:

DATE:

DEVOTIONAL NOTES:

BIBLE VERSES:

KEY POINTS:

BLESSINGS:

PRAYERS:

DATE:

DEVOTIONAL NOTES:

BIBLE VERSES:

KEY POINTS:

BLESSINGS:

PRAYERS:

DATE:

DEVOTIONAL NOTES:

BIBLE VERSES:

KEY POINTS:

BLESSINGS:

PRAYERS:

DATE:

DEVOTIONAL NOTES:

BIBLE VERSES:

KEY POINTS:

BLESSINGS:

PRAYERS:

DATE:

DEVOTIONAL NOTES:

BIBLE VERSES:

KEY POINTS:

BLESSINGS:

PRAYERS:

DATE:

DEVOTIONAL NOTES:

BIBLE VERSES:

KEY POINTS:

BLESSINGS:

PRAYERS:

DATE:

DEVOTIONAL NOTES:

BIBLE VERSES:

KEY POINTS:

BLESSINGS:

PRAYERS:

DATE:

DEVOTIONAL NOTES:

BIBLE VERSES:

KEY POINTS:

BLESSINGS:

PRAYERS:

DATE:

DEVOTIONAL NOTES:

BIBLE VERSES:

KEY POINTS:

BLESSINGS:

PRAYERS:

DATE:

DEVOTIONAL NOTES:

BIBLE VERSES:

KEY POINTS:

BLESSINGS:

PRAYERS:

DATE:

DEVOTIONAL NOTES:

BIBLE VERSES:

KEY POINTS:

BLESSINGS:

PRAYERS:

DATE:

DEVOTIONAL NOTES:

BIBLE VERSES:

KEY POINTS:

BLESSINGS:

PRAYERS:

DATE:

DEVOTIONAL NOTES:

BIBLE VERSES:

KEY POINTS:

BLESSINGS:

PRAYERS:

October

DATE:

DEVOTIONAL NOTES:

BIBLE VERSES:

KEY POINTS:

BLESSINGS:

PRAYERS:

DATE:

DEVOTIONAL NOTES:

BIBLE VERSES:

KEY POINTS:

BLESSINGS:

PRAYERS:

November

CALENDAR:

SUNDAY	MONDAY	TUESDAY	WEDNESDAY	THURSDAY	FRIDAY	SATURDAY

NOTES:

DATE:

DEVOTIONAL NOTES:

BIBLE VERSES:

KEY POINTS:

BLESSINGS:

PRAYERS:

DATE:

DEVOTIONAL NOTES:

BIBLE VERSES:

KEY POINTS:

BLESSINGS:

PRAYERS:

DATE:

DEVOTIONAL NOTES:

BIBLE VERSES:

KEY POINTS:

BLESSINGS:

PRAYERS:

DATE:

DEVOTIONAL NOTES:

BIBLE VERSES:

KEY POINTS:

BLESSINGS:

PRAYERS:

DATE:

DEVOTIONAL NOTES:

BIBLE VERSES:

KEY POINTS:

BLESSINGS:

PRAYERS:

November

DATE:

DEVOTIONAL NOTES:

BIBLE VERSES:

KEY POINTS:

BLESSINGS:

PRAYERS:

DATE:

DEVOTIONAL NOTES:

BIBLE VERSES:

KEY POINTS:

BLESSINGS:

PRAYERS:

DATE:

DEVOTIONAL NOTES:

BIBLE VERSES:

KEY POINTS:

BLESSINGS:

PRAYERS:

DATE:

DEVOTIONAL NOTES:

BIBLE VERSES:

KEY POINTS:

BLESSINGS:

PRAYERS:

November

DATE:

DEVOTIONAL NOTES:

BIBLE VERSES:

KEY POINTS:

BLESSINGS:

PRAYERS:

DATE:

DEVOTIONAL NOTES:

BIBLE VERSES:

KEY POINTS:

BLESSINGS:

PRAYERS:

November

DATE:

DEVOTIONAL NOTES:

BIBLE VERSES:

KEY POINTS:

BLESSINGS:

PRAYERS:

331

DATE:

DEVOTIONAL NOTES:

BIBLE VERSES:

KEY POINTS:

BLESSINGS:

PRAYERS:

DATE:

DEVOTIONAL NOTES:

BIBLE VERSES:

KEY POINTS:

BLESSINGS:

PRAYERS:

DATE:

DEVOTIONAL NOTES:

BIBLE VERSES:

KEY POINTS:

BLESSINGS:

PRAYERS:

November

DATE:

DEVOTIONAL NOTES:

BIBLE VERSES:

KEY POINTS:

BLESSINGS:

PRAYERS:

DATE:

DEVOTIONAL NOTES:

BIBLE VERSES:

KEY POINTS:

BLESSINGS:

PRAYERS:

November

DATE:

DEVOTIONAL NOTES:

BIBLE VERSES:

KEY POINTS:

BLESSINGS:

PRAYERS:

DATE:

DEVOTIONAL NOTES:

BIBLE VERSES:

KEY POINTS:

BLESSINGS:

PRAYERS:

November

DATE:

DEVOTIONAL NOTES:

BIBLE VERSES:

KEY POINTS:

BLESSINGS:

PRAYERS:

DATE:

DEVOTIONAL NOTES:

BIBLE VERSES:

KEY POINTS:

BLESSINGS:

PRAYERS:

DATE:

DEVOTIONAL NOTES:

BIBLE VERSES:

KEY POINTS:

BLESSINGS:

PRAYERS:

DATE:

DEVOTIONAL NOTES:

BIBLE VERSES:

KEY POINTS:

BLESSINGS:

PRAYERS:

DATE:

DEVOTIONAL NOTES:

BIBLE VERSES:

KEY POINTS:

BLESSINGS:

PRAYERS:

DATE:

DEVOTIONAL NOTES:

BIBLE VERSES:

KEY POINTS:

BLESSINGS:

PRAYERS:

November

DATE:

DEVOTIONAL NOTES:

BIBLE VERSES:

KEY POINTS:

BLESSINGS:

PRAYERS:

DATE:

DEVOTIONAL NOTES:

BIBLE VERSES:

KEY POINTS:

BLESSINGS:

PRAYERS:

DATE:

DEVOTIONAL NOTES:

BIBLE VERSES:

KEY POINTS:

BLESSINGS:

PRAYERS:

DATE:

DEVOTIONAL NOTES:

BIBLE VERSES:

KEY POINTS:

BLESSINGS:

PRAYERS:

November

DATE:

DEVOTIONAL NOTES:

BIBLE VERSES:

KEY POINTS:

BLESSINGS:

PRAYERS:

DATE:

DEVOTIONAL NOTES:

BIBLE VERSES:

KEY POINTS:

BLESSINGS:

PRAYERS:

December

CALENDAR:

SUNDAY	MONDAY	TUESDAY	WEDNESDAY	THURSDAY	FRIDAY	SATURDAY

NOTES:

DATE:

DEVOTIONAL NOTES:

BIBLE VERSES:

KEY POINTS:

BLESSINGS:

PRAYERS:

DATE:

DEVOTIONAL NOTES:

BIBLE VERSES:

KEY POINTS:

BLESSINGS:

PRAYERS:

DATE:

DEVOTIONAL NOTES:

BIBLE VERSES:

KEY POINTS:

BLESSINGS:

PRAYERS:

DATE:

DEVOTIONAL NOTES:

BIBLE VERSES:

KEY POINTS:

BLESSINGS:

PRAYERS:

DATE:

DEVOTIONAL NOTES:

BIBLE VERSES:

KEY POINTS:

BLESSINGS:

PRAYERS:

December

DATE:

DEVOTIONAL NOTES:

BIBLE VERSES:

KEY POINTS:

BLESSINGS:

PRAYERS:

DATE:

DEVOTIONAL NOTES:

BIBLE VERSES:

KEY POINTS:

BLESSINGS:

PRAYERS:

DATE:

DEVOTIONAL NOTES:

BIBLE VERSES:

KEY POINTS:

BLESSINGS:

PRAYERS:

DATE:

DEVOTIONAL NOTES:

BIBLE VERSES:

KEY POINTS:

BLESSINGS:

PRAYERS:

DATE:

DEVOTIONAL NOTES:

BIBLE VERSES:

KEY POINTS:

BLESSINGS:

PRAYERS:

DATE:

DEVOTIONAL NOTES:

BIBLE VERSES:

KEY POINTS:

BLESSINGS:

PRAYERS:

DATE:

DEVOTIONAL NOTES:

BIBLE VERSES:

KEY POINTS:

BLESSINGS:

PRAYERS:

DATE:

DEVOTIONAL NOTES:

BIBLE VERSES:

KEY POINTS:

BLESSINGS:

PRAYERS:

December

DATE:

DEVOTIONAL NOTES:

BIBLE VERSES:

KEY POINTS:

BLESSINGS:

PRAYERS:

DATE:

DEVOTIONAL NOTES:

BIBLE VERSES:

KEY POINTS:

BLESSINGS:

PRAYERS:

December

DATE:

DEVOTIONAL NOTES:

BIBLE VERSES:

KEY POINTS:

BLESSINGS:

PRAYERS:

DATE:

DEVOTIONAL NOTES:

BIBLE VERSES:

KEY POINTS:

BLESSINGS:

PRAYERS:

December

DATE:

DEVOTIONAL NOTES:

BIBLE VERSES:

KEY POINTS:

BLESSINGS:

PRAYERS:

DATE:

DEVOTIONAL NOTES:

BIBLE VERSES:

KEY POINTS:

BLESSINGS:

PRAYERS:

December

DATE:

DEVOTIONAL NOTES:

BIBLE VERSES:

KEY POINTS:

BLESSINGS:

PRAYERS:

DATE:

DEVOTIONAL NOTES:

BIBLE VERSES:

KEY POINTS:

BLESSINGS:

PRAYERS:

DATE:

DEVOTIONAL NOTES:

BIBLE VERSES:

KEY POINTS:

BLESSINGS:

PRAYERS:

DATE:

DEVOTIONAL NOTES:

BIBLE VERSES:

KEY POINTS:

BLESSINGS:

PRAYERS:

DATE:

DEVOTIONAL NOTES:

BIBLE VERSES:

KEY POINTS:

BLESSINGS:

PRAYERS:

DATE:

DEVOTIONAL NOTES:

BIBLE VERSES:

KEY POINTS:

BLESSINGS:

PRAYERS:

DATE:

DEVOTIONAL NOTES:

BIBLE VERSES:

KEY POINTS:

BLESSINGS:

PRAYERS:

DATE:

DEVOTIONAL NOTES:

BIBLE VERSES:

KEY POINTS:

BLESSINGS:

PRAYERS:

December

DATE:

DEVOTIONAL NOTES:

BIBLE VERSES:

KEY POINTS:

BLESSINGS:

PRAYERS:

DATE:

DEVOTIONAL NOTES:

BIBLE VERSES:

KEY POINTS:

BLESSINGS:

PRAYERS:

DATE:

DEVOTIONAL NOTES:

BIBLE VERSES:

KEY POINTS:

BLESSINGS:

PRAYERS:

DATE:

DEVOTIONAL NOTES:

BIBLE VERSES:

KEY POINTS:

BLESSINGS:

PRAYERS:

Life Applications

TOPIC:

BIBLE VERSES:

DATE:

TOPIC:

BIBLE VERSES:

DATE:

TOPIC:

BIBLE VERSES:

DATE:

TOPIC:

BIBLE VERSES:

DATE:

TOPIC:

BIBLE VERSES:

DATE:

TOPIC:

BIBLE VERSES:

DATE:

TOPIC:

BIBLE VERSES:

DATE:

TOPIC:

BIBLE VERSES:

DATE:

TOPIC:

BIBLE VERSES:

DATE:

TOPIC:

BIBLE VERSES:

DATE:

TOPIC:

BIBLE VERSES:

DATE:

TOPIC:

BIBLE VERSES:

DATE:

TOPIC:

BIBLE VERSES:

DATE:

TOPIC:

BIBLE VERSES:

DATE:

TOPIC:

BIBLE VERSES:

DATE:

TOPIC:

BIBLE VERSES:

DATE:

TOPIC:

BIBLE VERSES:

DATE:

TOPIC:

BIBLE VERSES:

DATE:

TOPIC:

BIBLE VERSES:

DATE:

TOPIC:

BIBLE VERSES:

DATE:

TOPIC:

BIBLE VERSES:

DATE:

TOPIC:

BIBLE VERSES:

DATE:

TOPIC:

BIBLE VERSES:

DATE:

TOPIC:

BIBLE VERSES:

DATE:

TOPIC:	BIBLE VERSES:
DATE:	

TOPIC:	BIBLE VERSES:
DATE:	

TOPIC:	BIBLE VERSES:
DATE:	

TOPIC:	BIBLE VERSES:
DATE:	

TOPIC:	BIBLE VERSES:
DATE:	

TOPIC:	BIBLE VERSES:
DATE:	

TOPIC:

BIBLE VERSES:

DATE:

TOPIC:

BIBLE VERSES:

DATE:

TOPIC:

BIBLE VERSES:

DATE:

TOPIC:

BIBLE VERSES:

DATE:

TOPIC:

BIBLE VERSES:

DATE:

TOPIC:

BIBLE VERSES:

DATE:

D

TOPIC:	BIBLE VERSES:
DATE:	

TOPIC:	BIBLE VERSES:
DATE:	

TOPIC:	BIBLE VERSES:
DATE:	

TOPIC:	BIBLE VERSES:
DATE:	

TOPIC:	BIBLE VERSES:
DATE:	

TOPIC:	BIBLE VERSES:
DATE:	

TOPIC:

BIBLE VERSES:

DATE:

TOPIC:

BIBLE VERSES:

DATE:

TOPIC:

BIBLE VERSES:

DATE:

TOPIC:

BIBLE VERSES:

DATE:

TOPIC:

BIBLE VERSES:

DATE:

TOPIC:

BIBLE VERSES:

DATE:

TOPIC:	BIBLE VERSES:
DATE:	

TOPIC:	BIBLE VERSES:
DATE:	

TOPIC:	BIBLE VERSES:
DATE:	

TOPIC:	BIBLE VERSES:
DATE:	

TOPIC:	BIBLE VERSES:
DATE:	

TOPIC:	BIBLE VERSES:
DATE:	

TOPIC:

BIBLE VERSES:

DATE:

TOPIC:

BIBLE VERSES:

DATE:

TOPIC:

BIBLE VERSES:

DATE:

TOPIC:

BIBLE VERSES:

DATE:

TOPIC:

BIBLE VERSES:

DATE:

TOPIC:

BIBLE VERSES:

DATE:

TOPIC:

BIBLE VERSES:

DATE:

TOPIC:

BIBLE VERSES:

DATE:

TOPIC:

BIBLE VERSES:

DATE:

TOPIC:

BIBLE VERSES:

DATE:

TOPIC:

BIBLE VERSES:

DATE:

TOPIC:

BIBLE VERSES:

DATE:

TOPIC:

BIBLE VERSES:

DATE:

TOPIC:

BIBLE VERSES:

DATE:

TOPIC:

BIBLE VERSES:

DATE:

TOPIC:

BIBLE VERSES:

DATE:

TOPIC:

BIBLE VERSES:

DATE:

TOPIC:

BIBLE VERSES:

DATE:

TOPIC:

DATE:

BIBLE VERSES:

TOPIC:

DATE:

BIBLE VERSES:

TOPIC:

DATE:

BIBLE VERSES:

TOPIC:

DATE:

BIBLE VERSES:

TOPIC:

DATE:

BIBLE VERSES:

TOPIC:

DATE:

BIBLE VERSES:

TOPIC:

BIBLE VERSES:

DATE:

TOPIC:

BIBLE VERSES:

DATE:

TOPIC:

BIBLE VERSES:

DATE:

TOPIC:

BIBLE VERSES:

DATE:

TOPIC:

BIBLE VERSES:

DATE:

TOPIC:

BIBLE VERSES:

DATE:

H

TOPIC:

BIBLE VERSES:

DATE:

TOPIC:

BIBLE VERSES:

DATE:

TOPIC:

BIBLE VERSES:

DATE:

TOPIC:

BIBLE VERSES:

DATE:

TOPIC:

BIBLE VERSES:

DATE:

TOPIC:

BIBLE VERSES:

DATE:

TOPIC:

BIBLE VERSES:

DATE:

TOPIC:

BIBLE VERSES:

DATE:

TOPIC:

BIBLE VERSES:

DATE:

TOPIC:

BIBLE VERSES:

DATE:

TOPIC:

BIBLE VERSES:

DATE:

TOPIC:

BIBLE VERSES:

DATE:

TOPIC:

BIBLE VERSES:

DATE:

TOPIC:

BIBLE VERSES:

DATE:

TOPIC:

BIBLE VERSES:

DATE:

TOPIC:

BIBLE VERSES:

DATE:

TOPIC:

BIBLE VERSES:

DATE:

TOPIC:

BIBLE VERSES:

DATE:

TOPIC:

BIBLE VERSES:

DATE:

TOPIC:

BIBLE VERSES:

DATE:

TOPIC:

BIBLE VERSES:

DATE:

TOPIC:

BIBLE VERSES:

DATE:

TOPIC:

BIBLE VERSES:

DATE:

TOPIC:

BIBLE VERSES:

DATE:

TOPIC:

BIBLE VERSES:

DATE:

TOPIC:

BIBLE VERSES:

DATE:

TOPIC:

BIBLE VERSES:

DATE:

TOPIC:

BIBLE VERSES:

DATE:

TOPIC:

BIBLE VERSES:

DATE:

TOPIC:

BIBLE VERSES:

DATE:

TOPIC:

BIBLE VERSES:

DATE:

TOPIC:

BIBLE VERSES:

DATE:

TOPIC:

BIBLE VERSES:

DATE:

TOPIC:

BIBLE VERSES:

DATE:

TOPIC:

BIBLE VERSES:

DATE:

TOPIC:

BIBLE VERSES:

DATE:

TOPIC:

BIBLE VERSES:

DATE:

TOPIC:

BIBLE VERSES:

DATE:

TOPIC:

BIBLE VERSES:

DATE:

TOPIC:

BIBLE VERSES:

DATE:

TOPIC:

BIBLE VERSES:

DATE:

TOPIC:

BIBLE VERSES:

DATE:

TOPIC:

BIBLE VERSES:

DATE:

TOPIC:

BIBLE VERSES:

DATE:

TOPIC:

BIBLE VERSES:

DATE:

TOPIC:

BIBLE VERSES:

DATE:

TOPIC:

BIBLE VERSES:

DATE:

TOPIC:

BIBLE VERSES:

DATE:

L

TOPIC:	BIBLE VERSES:
DATE:	

TOPIC:	BIBLE VERSES:
DATE:	

TOPIC:	BIBLE VERSES:
DATE:	

TOPIC:	BIBLE VERSES:
DATE:	

TOPIC:	BIBLE VERSES:
DATE:	

TOPIC:	BIBLE VERSES:
DATE:	

TOPIC:

BIBLE VERSES:

DATE:

TOPIC:

BIBLE VERSES:

DATE:

TOPIC:

BIBLE VERSES:

DATE:

TOPIC:

BIBLE VERSES:

DATE:

TOPIC:

BIBLE VERSES:

DATE:

TOPIC:

BIBLE VERSES:

DATE:

TOPIC:

DATE:

BIBLE VERSES:

TOPIC:

DATE:

BIBLE VERSES:

TOPIC:

DATE:

BIBLE VERSES:

TOPIC:

DATE:

BIBLE VERSES:

TOPIC:

DATE:

BIBLE VERSES:

TOPIC:

DATE:

BIBLE VERSES:

TOPIC:

BIBLE VERSES:

DATE:

TOPIC:

BIBLE VERSES:

DATE:

TOPIC:

BIBLE VERSES:

DATE:

TOPIC:

BIBLE VERSES:

DATE:

TOPIC:

BIBLE VERSES:

DATE:

TOPIC:

BIBLE VERSES:

DATE:

TOPIC:

BIBLE VERSES:

DATE:

TOPIC:

BIBLE VERSES:

DATE:

TOPIC:

BIBLE VERSES:

DATE:

TOPIC:

BIBLE VERSES:

DATE:

TOPIC:

BIBLE VERSES:

DATE:

TOPIC:

BIBLE VERSES:

DATE:

TOPIC:

BIBLE VERSES:

DATE:

TOPIC:

BIBLE VERSES:

DATE:

TOPIC:

BIBLE VERSES:

DATE:

TOPIC:

BIBLE VERSES:

DATE:

TOPIC:

BIBLE VERSES:

DATE:

TOPIC:

BIBLE VERSES:

DATE:

TOPIC:

BIBLE VERSES:

DATE:

TOPIC:

BIBLE VERSES:

DATE:

TOPIC:

BIBLE VERSES:

DATE:

TOPIC:

BIBLE VERSES:

DATE:

TOPIC:

BIBLE VERSES:

DATE:

TOPIC:

BIBLE VERSES:

DATE:

TOPIC:

BIBLE VERSES:

DATE:

TOPIC:

BIBLE VERSES:

DATE:

TOPIC:

BIBLE VERSES:

DATE:

TOPIC:

BIBLE VERSES:

DATE:

TOPIC:

BIBLE VERSES:

DATE:

TOPIC:

BIBLE VERSES:

DATE:

TOPIC:

BIBLE VERSES:

DATE:

TOPIC:

BIBLE VERSES:

DATE:

TOPIC:

BIBLE VERSES:

DATE:

TOPIC:

BIBLE VERSES:

DATE:

TOPIC:

BIBLE VERSES:

DATE:

TOPIC:

BIBLE VERSES:

DATE:

TOPIC:

DATE:

BIBLE VERSES:

TOPIC:

DATE:

BIBLE VERSES:

TOPIC:

DATE:

BIBLE VERSES:

TOPIC:

DATE:

BIBLE VERSES:

TOPIC:

DATE:

BIBLE VERSES:

TOPIC:

DATE:

BIBLE VERSES:

TOPIC:	BIBLE VERSES:
DATE:	

TOPIC:	BIBLE VERSES:
DATE:	

TOPIC:	BIBLE VERSES:
DATE:	

TOPIC:	BIBLE VERSES:
DATE:	

TOPIC:	BIBLE VERSES:
DATE:	

TOPIC:	BIBLE VERSES:
DATE:	

TOPIC:

BIBLE VERSES:

DATE:

TOPIC:

BIBLE VERSES:

DATE:

TOPIC:

BIBLE VERSES:

DATE:

TOPIC:

BIBLE VERSES:

DATE:

TOPIC:

BIBLE VERSES:

DATE:

TOPIC:

BIBLE VERSES:

DATE:

TOPIC:

BIBLE VERSES:

DATE:

TOPIC:

BIBLE VERSES:

DATE:

TOPIC:

BIBLE VERSES:

DATE:

TOPIC:

BIBLE VERSES:

DATE:

TOPIC:

BIBLE VERSES:

DATE:

TOPIC:

BIBLE VERSES:

DATE:

TOPIC:

BIBLE VERSES:

DATE:

TOPIC:

BIBLE VERSES:

DATE:

TOPIC:

BIBLE VERSES:

DATE:

TOPIC:

BIBLE VERSES:

DATE:

TOPIC:

BIBLE VERSES:

DATE:

TOPIC:

BIBLE VERSES:

DATE:

TOPIC:	BIBLE VERSES:
DATE:	

TOPIC:	BIBLE VERSES:
DATE:	

TOPIC:	BIBLE VERSES:
DATE:	

TOPIC:	BIBLE VERSES:
DATE:	

TOPIC:	BIBLE VERSES:
DATE:	

TOPIC:	BIBLE VERSES:
DATE:	

TOPIC:

BIBLE VERSES:

DATE:

TOPIC:

BIBLE VERSES:

DATE:

TOPIC:

BIBLE VERSES:

DATE:

TOPIC:

BIBLE VERSES:

DATE:

TOPIC:

BIBLE VERSES:

DATE:

TOPIC:

BIBLE VERSES:

DATE:

TOPIC:

DATE:

BIBLE VERSES:

TOPIC:

DATE:

BIBLE VERSES:

TOPIC:

DATE:

BIBLE VERSES:

TOPIC:

DATE:

BIBLE VERSES:

TOPIC:

DATE:

BIBLE VERSES:

TOPIC:

DATE:

BIBLE VERSES:

TOPIC:

DATE:

BIBLE VERSES:

TOPIC:

DATE:

BIBLE VERSES:

TOPIC:

DATE:

BIBLE VERSES:

TOPIC:

DATE:

BIBLE VERSES:

TOPIC:

DATE:

BIBLE VERSES:

TOPIC:

DATE:

BIBLE VERSES:

U

TOPIC:	BIBLE VERSES:
DATE:	

TOPIC:	BIBLE VERSES:
DATE:	

TOPIC:	BIBLE VERSES:
DATE:	

TOPIC:	BIBLE VERSES:
DATE:	

TOPIC:	BIBLE VERSES:
DATE:	

TOPIC:	BIBLE VERSES:
DATE:	

TOPIC:

BIBLE VERSES:

DATE:

TOPIC:

BIBLE VERSES:

DATE:

TOPIC:

BIBLE VERSES:

DATE:

TOPIC:

BIBLE VERSES:

DATE:

TOPIC:

BIBLE VERSES:

DATE:

TOPIC:

BIBLE VERSES:

DATE:

V

TOPIC:	BIBLE VERSES:
DATE:	

TOPIC:	BIBLE VERSES:
DATE:	

TOPIC:	BIBLE VERSES:
DATE:	

TOPIC:	BIBLE VERSES:
DATE:	

TOPIC:	BIBLE VERSES:
DATE:	

TOPIC:	BIBLE VERSES:
DATE:	

TOPIC:

BIBLE VERSES:

DATE:

TOPIC:

BIBLE VERSES:

DATE:

TOPIC:

BIBLE VERSES:

DATE:

TOPIC:

BIBLE VERSES:

DATE:

TOPIC:

BIBLE VERSES:

DATE:

TOPIC:

BIBLE VERSES:

DATE:

TOPIC:

DATE:

BIBLE VERSES:

TOPIC:

DATE:

BIBLE VERSES:

TOPIC:

DATE:

BIBLE VERSES:

TOPIC:

DATE:

BIBLE VERSES:

TOPIC:

DATE:

BIBLE VERSES:

TOPIC:

DATE:

BIBLE VERSES:

TOPIC:

BIBLE VERSES:

DATE:

TOPIC:

BIBLE VERSES:

DATE:

TOPIC:

BIBLE VERSES:

DATE:

TOPIC:

BIBLE VERSES:

DATE:

TOPIC:

BIBLE VERSES:

DATE:

TOPIC:

BIBLE VERSES:

DATE:

TOPIC:

BIBLE VERSES:

DATE:

TOPIC:

BIBLE VERSES:

DATE:

TOPIC:

BIBLE VERSES:

DATE:

TOPIC:

BIBLE VERSES:

DATE:

TOPIC:

BIBLE VERSES:

DATE:

TOPIC:

BIBLE VERSES:

DATE:

TOPIC:

BIBLE VERSES:

DATE:

TOPIC:

BIBLE VERSES:

DATE:

TOPIC:

BIBLE VERSES:

DATE:

TOPIC:

BIBLE VERSES:

DATE:

TOPIC:

BIBLE VERSES:

DATE:

TOPIC:

BIBLE VERSES:

DATE:

CPSIA information can be obtained
at www.ICGtesting.com
Printed in the USA
LVHW060801080123
736685LV00004B/6

9 781400 330942